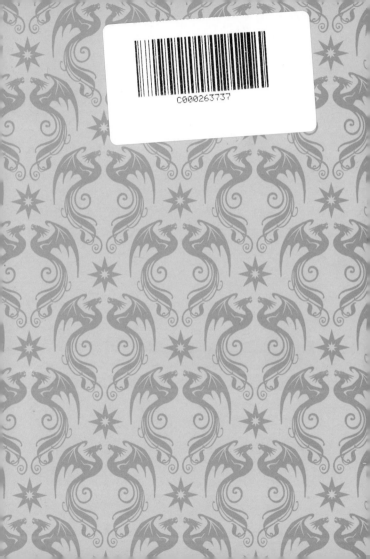

# SPELL BOUND

Illustrated by Anne Stokes
Written by John Woodward & Anne Stokes

First published in 2013 by Anne Stokes Collection Limited
Third Edition published in 2019

www.annestokes.com

Printed in the UK

ISBN 978-0-9569446-2-7

Distributed by Eastgate Resource Limited
www.eastgateresource.co.uk

In spiritu et veritate
ibi est magicae in omnibus

# BE WARNED

Before you begin weaving spells, what you give out in magic returns to you threefold. The energy you put into your spells increases and grows as it is released, so be careful what you wish for because you may have to live with the consequences for a long time. However, by asking with sincerity, you ask from the right place, from the heart, and this is the true power that you hold within you. It is important not to be fearful of magic, but be humble.

There are many roads to enlightenment and it is up to each of us to find our own path. As we strive to seek solutions and find guidance we can use simple things around us to help focus our minds and harness the powers of positivity and light. The artworks in this book are here to inspire the mind and creativity of the soul. In many ways the world of fantasy parallels our own and symbolises our emotions and situations.

The spells in this book do not have to be followed to the letter but used as a guide to channel positive thoughts and outcomes.

We wish you well on your journey of discovery into this Spellbound realm of fantasy.

# PREPARING FOR SPELLWEAVING

The most important element to performing a successful spell is belief. The second is feeling; the more concentrated positive effort you fill your spell with, the more potent your spell shall be. To build your concentrated energy, you may try energetic breathing. To do this, do as follows:

1. Make sure your feet are firmly set upon the ground, shoulder width apart, and feel their contact with the earth. With your hands resting on your stomach, take a few deep breaths, deep in your stomach, this is to ground yourself.
2. Place both hands just below the sternum. Begin to breathe, not too deeply, but slow and with concentration.
3. On each inward breath, breathe through your nose, and draw golden light into yourself. Hold the breath for a short time and feel your heart opening. On each outward breath, breathe through your mouth.
4. Breathe this way until you feel energized and wide awake. Then rest your hands on the heart for a few moments, breathing normally.

# THE PLEDGE

*To prepare for casting a spell, begin by inner cleansing, your mind must be focused and full of energy. You should also take the spellweaver's pledge that the magic spell you about to create shall be for the higher good.*

*To begin with, place your hands on your heart and ask that you be filled with the light of love. Imagine the golden light and feelings of love filling your heart and then your whole body.*

*Let the light begin to radiate out in all directions, so that you are surrounded by an aura of its golden rays. Raise your arms so that the palms of your hands are facing the sky, as though you are receiving the light. Now say the pledge and then slowly bring your arms down to your sides.*

I call upon the divine will of the universe,
To send a blessing upon my heart,
So that I may be filled with the light
of love and truth in all that I do.

I pledge that from this day,
I will do my best to harm none with
my thoughts, words or deeds.

I pledge that any magic I perform
will be for the highest good of all.
So mote it be !

# TALISMANS

Traditionally a talisman is an object marked with magic signs or depiction of a mythical creature. It is believed to confer on its bearer supernatural powers or protection. Every culture in human history has offered its followers' small decorative objects which purpose is to do anything ranging between healing, protection or success. Today, you may take any small decorative object and empower it as your own talisman (see page 74). Here are some examples and their meanings.

Sun Phoenix
for Optimism

Draca Stella
Good Fortune
through Friendship

Lunar Unicorn
for Making Good Decisions

Divine Pegasus
for Inspiration

Triskel Oak
For personal growth

Angel of Life
For True Love

# BOOK OF SHADOWS

*A Book of Shadows is used to store information,
such as spells you use more frequently or notes, such as which incense,
talisman etc. you prefer. It doesn't always have to be handwritten; indeed
you could use a computer to store information. However, bear in mind that
it is considered a sacred tool and should be respected as such. If you copy
your spells and rituals into your book by hand – this will not only transfer
energy to the writer, but it also helps you to memorize the contents.
Make sure you write legibly enough that you'll be able to read
your notes whilst reciting your spells.*

*To make your Book of Shadows, begin with a blank notebook. The
size is entirely personal and doesn't need to be a large and heavy tome
as is always depicted in television series or movies. It could be small
enough to carry on your person. You could even use a ring binder so
items can be added as needed. If you use this style of B.O.S, you can
use sheet protectors as well, which is ideal for preventing candle wax
and other things from getting on the pages. Simply write,
"The Book of Shadows
of [ your name]" on the
front page.*

# SPELL ENHANCEMENT

To enhance the power or your spell and set the mood you can use some of the following...

*Magic circle:* A magic circle is a space made to create a sacred area that will contain energy and serve as a form of protection. It can be physically marked, by things such as a line of salt, or a chalk drawing on the ground, or a length of cord laid around. It can also just be visualised. Creating a magic circle is known as casting a circle. The four cardinal directions can be marked by drawn symbols or objects, such as with four candles. Quarter candles can be colours that correspond to the four elements. Yellow for air placed in the east, red for fire in the south, blue for water in the west and green for earth in the north. The circle is usually closed by its creator after they have finished by taking in the energy with whatever tool they have used to draw it.

*Salt:* To purify a space, you can make a salt circle. Stand facing east, and cast it in the four directions going clockwise. You can also place salt in each of the four corners of a room for protection or a line across a door way to neutralise energy and ward off unwanted spirits.

*Candles:* One of the simplest forms of magical enhancement is candle burning. The candles you use should be new and unused so the spell can begin without being tarnished by vibrations picked up from past uses. The colour of the candle chosen can also enhance the purpose of the spell.

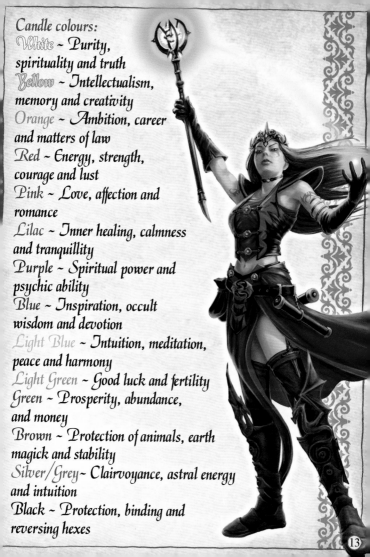

Candle colours:

White ~ Purity, spirituality and truth

Yellow ~ Intellectualism, memory and creativity

Orange ~ Ambition, career and matters of law

Red ~ Energy, strength, courage and lust

Pink ~ Love, affection and romance

Lilac ~ Inner healing, calmness and tranquillity

Purple ~ Spiritual power and psychic ability

Blue ~ Inspiration, occult wisdom and devotion

Light Blue ~ Intuition, meditation, peace and harmony

Light Green ~ Good luck and fertility

Green ~ Prosperity, abundance, and money

Brown ~ Protection of animals, earth magick and stability

Silver/Grey~ Clairvoyance, astral energy and intuition

Black ~ Protection, binding and reversing hexes

# INCENSE AND ITS MEANINGS

*Since ancient times, Incense has been used as a way to carry prayers and hope to the Gods and create a pleasant environment for humans to connect spiritually. In some of the spells we suggest a particular fragrance to use, but in the end, it's all a personal preference. Here are just a few examples of the associations incense has with spells.*

**Blueberry** ~ Keep unwanted influences away from your home and property

**Carnations** ~ A sweet floral scent used for healing

**Cherry** ~ Will attract and stimulate love

**Cinnamon** ~ Use to gain wealth and success

**Coconut** ~ To be burnt for protection and purification

**Frangipani** ~ To brighten your home with friendship and love

**Frankincense** ~ To stimulate positive vibrations

**Honeysuckle** ~ For good health, luck, and psychic power

**Jasmine** ~ Increase psychic ability and good luck, especially in matters relating to love

**Lavender** ~ Induce rest & sleep, divination and to attract love, especially of a man

**Lotus** ~ Find inner peace, outer harmony and to aid in meditation

**Musk** ~ Burn for courage, vitality and to heighten sensual passion

**Myrrh** ~ Ancient incense for protection, healing, purification and spirituality

**Passionflower** ~ Its sweet scent will soothe troubles and aid in sleep

**Patchouli** ~ Earthy scent used in money and attraction spells

**Pine** ~ Burn for strength, and to reverse negative energies

**Rose** ~ For love magic as well as to return calm energies to the home

**Sandalwood** ~ Delicious scent used to heal and protect, also for purification

**Spice** ~ A fiery scent to be charged for any magic

**Strawberry** ~ For love, luck and friendship

**Orange Peel** ~ Burned for luck, love, money and weddings

**Vanilla** ~ Stimulate amorous appetites, increase psychic ability and enhance memory

# PHASES OF THE MOON

Lunar phases occur because the Moon revolves around the Earth and one side of the Moon always faces the Sun, and hence is illuminated by it. The cycle takes approximately 29.5 days, shorter than most calendar months; therefore the dates of the phases vary. When there are two Full Moons occurring in one calendar month, the second one is called a Blue Moon. This only happens every two or three years.

The Moon affects the Earth and the cycles of nature. The tides of the sea are the rise and fall of sea levels caused by the gravitational forces exerted by the Moon and the Sun and the rotation of the Earth. Many cultures believe that the moon can affect our emotions and the full moon in particular can affect people's consciousness, emotions, and behaviour. There is also a belief that working rituals at the time of different phases of the moon can bring about physical or psychological change or transformation. Historically these rituals have been practised at the time of the full moon, and to a lesser extent the new moon. Legendary creatures such as Lycanthropes (werewolves) are said to transform at the time of the full moon and then possess extraordinary strength and speed. Spells and rituals may work to a lesser or greater extend depending on the current phase of the moon. For extra power spells can be done on a clear night when the moon is full and the lunar power can be harnessed to its most full effect.

The Triple Goddess is formed of the maiden, mother and crone, as they represent the cycle of life. The symbol for the goddess consists of three phases of the moon. Waxing, full, and waning.

# FESTIVALS

The Eight Sabbats form the Wheel of the Year. A never ending circle, they celebrate the seasons, cycles of growth and life. Some of the dates shown are for the northern hemisphere and vary, as the seasons do, in the southern hemisphere.

*Samhain:* The most important festival which marks the beginning and ending of the wheel. A time when the veil between the living and spirit worlds is thin.

*Yule:* The Winter Solstice is the shortest day and longest night of the year. The festival of the rebirth of the sun.

*Imbolc:* Marks the first signs of spring. Symbolised by a maiden and light.

*Oestara:* The Spring Equinox when day and night are equal. A celebration of spring and the awakening of the land after winter.

*Beltane:* The second most important festival. A fire and fertility festival. A common time for hand~fasting (form of wedding).

*Litha:* The Summer Solstice is the longest day and shortest night. The Sun is at the peak of its power but is now about to decline as the Holly King takes over from the Oak King.

*Lammas:* Celebrated at the first harvest. It is linked with sacrifice and death. Symbolised by the Corn King.

*Madron:* The Autumn Equinox when day and night are equal. A time to seek balance within yourself.

Samhain

31st October

All Hallows Eve

Madron

21st September

Autumn Equinox

Yule

21st December

Winter Solstice

Imbolc

2nd February

Festival of Brigit

Lammas

1st August

Loaf-mass

Lughnasadh

Litha

21st June

Summer Solstice

Beltane

1st May

May Day

Ostara

21st March

Spring Equinox

As the woods
in which we played
Together you and
I have grown,
May our friendship
never fade
And with love
our bond is sewn.

# CELEBRATING A FRIENDSHIP

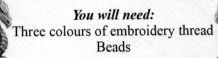

### You will need:
Three colours of embroidery thread
Beads

*Here we use three different colours so you can easily see what is going on.*

*Begin by tying a knot at the end, then taking the far left thread and passing it over the top of the lace next to it. Now take the far right thread and pass it over the lace next that. Continue crossing this way until the desired length is reached. Beads can be added at any middle point in the braiding.*

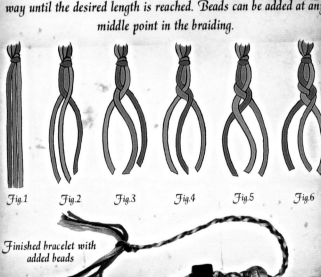

Fig.1    Fig.2    Fig.3    Fig.4    Fig.5    Fig.6

*Finished bracelet with added beads*

This spell bonds a friendship
whilst at the same time giving you
something creative to do. Think about the person
you are making the bracelet for; what is their favourite
colour, what element (*fire, earth, air or water*) are they?

These are things that can be integrated into the plaiting,
either by the colour of the thread or in the beads chosen.
Take your embroidery thread and begin to plait (*see the
opposite page for a how-to-do-guide if you're unsure*),
use your own wrist as a guide to how long you think it
should be. When you get to approximately the middle
add a bead (the first represents you). Plait a little more
then add their bead and at this point say the following
three times:

Through my hands may my love flow
And seep into each braid I bind,
May the wearer of this token know
Always in me a true friend find.

When you present your bracelet, it must be you that
ties the knot as this the final act in the spell.
A long and lasting friendship
will ensue.

*Amidst*
*the isolation of these*
*sepulchres cold*
*I seek perfection among*
*rambling briars,*
*Forever a symbol of*
*love's truth told*
*A fitting place for*
*those they*
*honour.*

# ATTRACTING LOVE

***You will need:***
Dried rose petals.
A length of thin ribbon
Incense (*rose*).

The rose has been a symbol for love since ancient times. Indeed, it is written that it was the Greek Gods that were responsible for its creation. Chloris, the Goddess of flowers created rose by giving life to lifeless body of a nymph. Aphrodite, the Goddess of love gave her beauty and Dionysus, the God of wine presented her nectar to give her sweet scent and the three Graces gave her charm, brightness and joy. Henceforth, it became the one true symbol of lovers.

This spell may
be used at any time to attract a
lover but it's at its most potent if performed
on a Friday. Light one or two sticks of incense. Onto
a warm bath, scatter dried rose petals; enter the water
whilst holding your piece of ribbon. Relax in the rose
infused water and chant the spell three times whilst tying
three knots in the ribbon, one for each spell you chant.
The first knot is for you, the second for your new lover
and a third for the love you shall share together.

I have pure passion in my heart
It is now time for love to start

Venus, bless my longing heart's quest
And send to me a love that's blest

I need this love and I will be true
This, Venus is my pledge to you

I chant this spell three times three
The spell is cast, so mote it be!

Keep the ribbon with you until you meet
your new love, then, bury it under a
rose bush so that your love will
grow and blossom.

By the power
within my sword
I absorb the elements
all around me,
My winged companion
of the sky is lord
Together they will
keep the land
below free.

# GAIN COURAGE

**You will need:**
A pebble or small stone
Incense (*musk*)

石 石 石 石

Forging a sword uses heat (*steel becomes red hot around 1200 - 1500 degrees Fahrenheit*) to bring the material to a flexible state. It is then hammered to shape, using hammer and anvil, together with specialized

*A wyvern or wivern is a legendary winged creature with a dragon's head, reptilian body, two legs (sometimes none) and a barbed tail.*

set of tools depending on the particular technique. There are a variety of forging techniques for sword making and many variations upon those.

In times of stress we all
could do with help to conquer it.
This spell will help give to give you just
that. You will need a small pebble, something that
feels comfortable in the hand. This spell will harness
the power of the fire that lies at the heart of all stones;
power that was forged millions of years ago when the
earth began. It is the same power from the fire that gives
the dragon both its strength and courage. Leave the
stone somewhere cold, maybe outside overnight or even
in the fridge? Take the cold stone and clasp it tightly
between both hands. Feel the coldness depart as the
warmth of your body heats it. Concentrate and imagine a
fire within the held pebble and say the following aloud:

*Element of fire that lies within*
*This rock I hold let magic begin,*

*To my spirit let dragons breath flow*
*Allow your courage within me to grow,*

*I say aloud three times three*
*Courage is mine so mote it be,*

The once dormant fire is now reborn within the stone
and is now your personal symbol for the courage
you shall find within yourself. Keep it safe
and in times of need, hold it close
to your heart and feels its
warmth and comfort.

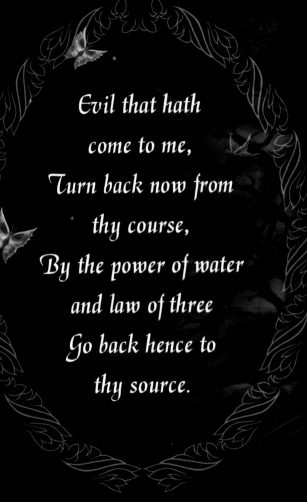

Evil that hath
come to me,
Turn back now from
thy course,
By the power of water
and law of three
Go back hence to
thy source.

# TO DISPEL A BAD EXPERIENCE
# OR RECURRING BAD DREAMS

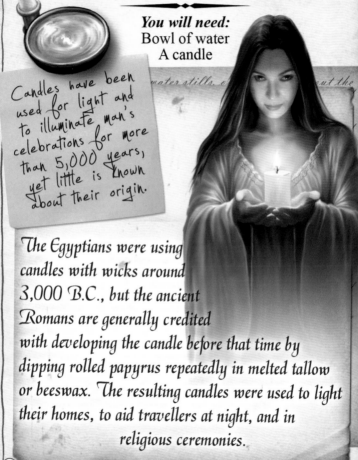

***You will need:***
Bowl of water
A candle

Candles have been used for light and to illuminate man's celebrations for more than 5,000 years, yet little is known about their origin.

The Egyptians were using candles with wicks around 3,000 B.C., but the ancient Romans are generally credited with developing the candle before that time by dipping rolled papyrus repeatedly in melted tallow or beeswax. The resulting candles were used to light their homes, to aid travellers at night, and in religious ceremonies.

To be done at night
or in a darkened room.
Position the candle so that you can see the
flame reflected in the water. Concentrate your mind
on the flames reflection and imagine it containing the
subject you wish to dispel. Say aloud the
following verse:

Flame, flame that now burns before me
Absorb the thoughts I don't want to be

I ask you direct to aid in this quest
And to finally lay my worries to rest

Reflections cannot hurt nor cause me fear
So now disperse and be gone from here.

As you say the last line disturb the water with your finger
so that the reflection is broken. Then, before the water
stills, blow out the candle. In doing this you will
have dispelled any worries that may have
been troubling you.

May

the petals from

this sweet rose

And the tears from

my saddened eyes,

Together combined banish

all doubts and woes

Bring my one true

love by next

moonrise.

# FOR A LOVED ONE FAR AWAY

***You will need:***
A small feather
Incense (*vanilla*)

When you find a feather in your path, know that your Angels are with you!

Beside from the energy that person brings into the object, feathers hold certain natural abilities too.

Feathers can be used in spells to focus ones concentration. When used for magical deeds, the energy output is relative to the energy that is used by the person performing the spell. Therefore, the stronger your conviction in what you are performing, the greater the results. Feathers represent the element of air, and as such, are excellent for spells requiring undertakings over distances. Each feather holds different qualities, dependent on the type of bird it came from, the colour and where it was found.

Light the incense
to focus your mind. Place a cushion on
the floor, then, sitting on it cross-legged;
place the feather into the palm of your hand.
Close your eyes and empty your mind of all
thoughts except one, the person that is away
from you at this moment. Now, remember a place
that you both shared together. Think of the
sights, sounds, smells of this place and of the
whole experience that you both felt there. Feel
that closeness you shared on this
occasion and focus on it whilst thinking of where
that person is at that moment. Feel that closeness
and imagine them receiving your love as though
it were a gift being handed over in person.

The feather that you held in your hand is now a
strong conduit for the experience you've just
felt; keep it safe in a box or pouch. To increase its
power for subsequent spells, keep it with a small
item relating to that person.

In

shimmering splendour

and the purest of pure

This gentle creature a

symbol of hope,

A blessing granted of

his timeless allure

Instil in us your strength

that we may

cope.

# GUIDANCE IN FINDING THE TRUE PATH

***You will need:***
A white candle
Incense (*lavender*)

Further to the story reported earlier this week regarding the strange white animal seen on Bodmin moor; well this reporter has seen it with my own eyes. All I can say is that from the distance my guide and I were at, the beast was nothing more than a unicorn, yes, a real life unicorn. The photographic evidence is being developed as I write this brief but world shattering piece of news. As soon as we have it then you will all be the first to see and believe in this wondrous and most beautiful of animals.

record breaking tee

The unicorn is a legendary animal from European folklore that resembles a white horse with a large, pointed, spiralling horn projecting from its forehead, sometimes a goat's beard and cloven hooves. First mentioned by the ancient Greeks, it became the most important imaginary animal of the Middle Ages and Renaissance when it was commonly described as an extremely wild woodland creature, a symbol of purity and grace, which could only be captured by a virgin.

Light a white candle
and some incense, preferably lavender
and sit peacefully and undisturbed. Let your mind
bath in the purity of the flickering candle light. Clear
all thoughts and allow the aroma of the incense to bring
about a state of calm. Imagine yourself in a quiet sunlit
forest glade deep within a mystical wood. Now, think of
the issue that is troubling you and the various solutions
that may be possible, as if they are separate paths leading
out of the glade. Recite the following verse and imagine a
white unicorn standing in the centre of the glade.

## Vision of beauty and grace
## I brought you to this place,
## Now aid me and help to see
## The path that's right for me.

If you are fortunate the unicorn will walk away
down the path that is the right choice for
you to follow.

In

glorious splendour

is our union bound

Together we are

stronger by far,

A symbol to all of a

friendship found

Look upon us to see

how suited we

are.

# KINSHIP WITH A LOVED ONE

***You will need:***
A locket

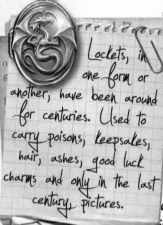

Lockets, in one form or another, have been around for centuries. Used to carry poisons, keepsakes, hair, ashes, good luck charms and only in the last century, pictures.

The Algonquian tribes of Native Americans had many different names for the Full Moon through the year, reflecting their connection with nature and the seasons, hunting, fishing, and farming.

The Moon is our closest cosmic neighbour and although it's much smaller than the sun, it strongly affects the Earth. In terms of gravitation, the moon exerts two and a half times the gravitational pull of the sun. Its influences are felt by every living thing on our planet and not just in terms of the tides. These lunar influences are a vital factor in the Earth's ability to support life. In Wicca she is worshipped as Grandmother Moon, because without the Moon, life may never have evolved here.

This will join
you and a loved one in a protective spell.
It can be a lover, family member, friend or pet.
Place into the locket a small picture of whoever
you have chosen. This image will become the
psychic bond that will both share. Close the
locket and hold it in a clenched fist, then lay
your other hand flat and palm down on top. You
will feel warmth arising from the locket, focus
on it whilst saying the following three times:

Standing beneath the mystic moon

Holding tight to this trinket bright,

I ask that your protection may soon

From this night forth our souls unite.

*(Say the following only once)*

By the power of three grant my request

So mote it be!

Now you can wear the locket close to your
heart in the full knowledge that by the
power of the moon you
are both in its
protection.

This
winter's night bright
under cold moon
A message I do
send to thee,
On parchment written
my magical rune
To ask for your sweet
love truly.

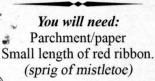

# LOVE SPELL

***You will need:***
Parchment/paper
Small length of red ribbon.
(sprig of mistletoe)

The tradition of hanging mistletoe is decidedly pagan in origin and dates back to Scandinavian mythology when Baldur, god of peace was slain by Loki, god of destruction with an arrow made from mistletoe. Outraged by the injustice of Baldur's death the other gods and goddesses demanded his life be restored. As a token of thanks, Baldur's mother, Frigga, hung mistletoe and promised to kiss all who passed beneath it, thus establishing the symbolism of love, peace and forgiveness that is now associated with it.

✳ Mistletoe plant, dried and powdered, particularly if it came from an oak tree was said to be good for epilepsy and to cure "love sickness" and other uses included cures for debility and paralytic weakness.

✳ Burning a piece of paper with your lover's name written on it can have them burning with desire for you.

Take your
piece of parchment
and write on it, in red ink, the name
of the person you desire. Fold it three times and
tie with the red ribbon saying the following verse
three times:

Let this ink represent my blood
That I spill onto this page unwounded

This name is emblazed on my heart
Let it stay there and never depart

I desire your arms to hold me always
Venus, grant me this I praise

I speak this spell for thee
It is now cast, so mote it be!

Keep the tied parchment under your pillow. Then for the
next three days, hold it in your clenched hand and repeat
the verse. After the third day, remove the ribbon and
safely burn the parchment. For added power to this spell,
a sprig of mistletoe can be bound to the parchment
by the ribbon.

In mystic glade as
the moon shines bright
Amidst the rambling
briars of old,
She illuminates all
with wondrous light
The virtues of her
magic are extolled.

# PROTECTION FROM EVIL

***You will need:***
Three candles
Paper
A piece of ribbon
Incense (*coconut*).

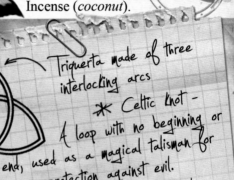

Triquerta made of three interlocking arcs

✳ Celtic Knot –
A loop with no beginning or end, used as a magical talisman for protection against evil.

✳ Power of three – maiden, mother and crone

Without a doubt, the most commonly encountered 'protection from evil charm' is the horseshoe. Believed to repel witches from entering your house, as well as to bring good luck to all that pass under it. The horseshoe must be hung above your front door and may either be nailed facing up or down. This belief originated from 16th century English folklore and horseshoes continue to greet visitors to homes around the world.

The atmosphere
of the room needs to be relaxed
and comfortable, so try lighting some incense
before performing this spell? On a piece of paper
draw a triquerta symbol. With your index finger
trace over the image continuously whilst reciting
the following:

I hereby invoke the power of three
To enter my life and protect me,

In my heart their strength shall reside
All evil forces from now to be denied,

I recite this spell three times three
evil shall harm so may it be,

Once you have recited the above three times, roll
up the piece of paper. Take the piece of ribbon and
tie three small knots into it and wrap and tie it
around the paper. Keep it now in a safe place and
repeat the spell
in times of need.

In these waters of
purity and beginning
You shall start
your life anew,
For your spirit is
still transcending
Find the strength
within to pursue.

# PURIFICATION SPELL

*You will need:*
Candles
Incense (*myrrh*)
A piece of Quartz crystal.

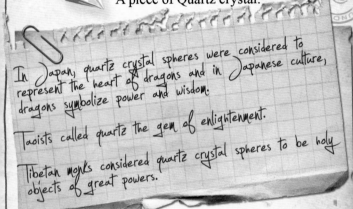

In Japan, quartz crystal spheres were considered to represent the heart of dragons and in Japanese culture, dragons symbolize power and wisdom.

Taoists called quartz the gem of enlightenment.

Tibetan monks considered quartz crystal spheres to be holy objects of great powers.

Quartz crystal symbolizes balance and perfection and as a healing stone is considered to be the strongest. It generates strong vibrations that cleanse the organs and instils a harmony to the body. It is said to absorb negative energy and helps the balanced expression of emotion, thought and desire; as well as enhancing psychic abilities.

After running yourself
a warm bath, place several candles
safely around the bath. Light one or two sticks of
incense. Climb into the bath; holding the quartz
crystal under the water level, close your eyes and
meditate yourself into a calm and relaxed state. Then,
imagine all the bad energy flowing along your body and
focus it towards your fingers holding the crystal. Keep
holding until you feel the negative energy leave and at
this point let go of the crystal to let it fall to then bottom
of the bath. Now you can exit the bath and release the
water away *(making sure to retrieve the crystal)* and
with it will be all the pent-up negative
energy and you will feel
refreshed and positive.

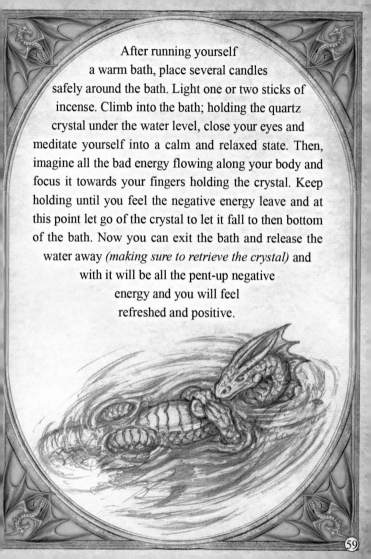

Looking glass
what is this
in front of me?
Captor and portrayer of
my very soul,
Am I to believe
the vision I see
This purity that here
you extol?

# REVEAL ᴛʜᴇ TRUTH

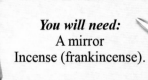

***You will need:***
A mirror
Incense (frankincense).

A common superstition is that someone who breaks a mirror will receive seven years of bad luck. The reason for this is that the mirror is believed to reflect part of the soul and therefore, breaking a mirror will break part of the soul. However, the soul is said to regenerate every seven years, consequently coming back unbroken.

In legend, a vampire has no reflection in mirrors because it is an undead creature and has already lost its soul.

The earliest forms of manufactured mirrors were actually pieces of polished stone, predominantly obsidian, a naturally occurring volcanic glass. Examples of obsidian mirrors found in Anatolia (now modern-day Turkey) have been dated to around 6000 BC. Examples too of polished stone mirrors from Central and South America date from around 2000 BC onwards.

The mirror reflects
the world back to us and the power
of reflection can be used in a spell to reveal
the truth. Think about an issue or problem that is
bothering you. One that is hard to see the correct
course of action. Sit quietly in a room; light some
incense, ideally frankincense, to calm and clear your
mind. Hold this page up facing a mirror, then, reading
the reflection recite the following verse:

Mirror I look in to you to see
Options that are eluding me,
Aid me to see a path so true
That I may face them all anew,

Breathe
deeply and again
examine the
possibilities before
you. This reflective
state should aid your
discovery of the
true path.

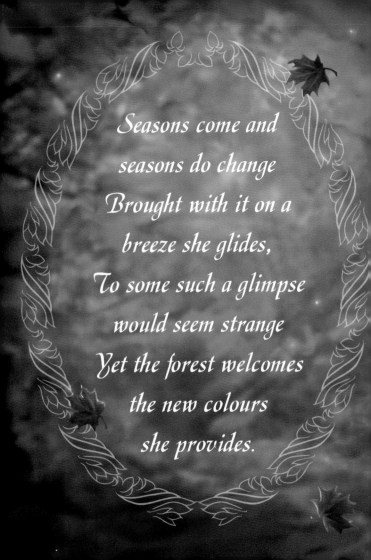

Seasons come and
seasons do change
Brought with it on a
breeze she glides,
To some such a glimpse
would seem strange
Yet the forest welcomes
the new colours
she provides.

# SAFE JOURNEY

**You will need:**
A falling leaf

*A dryad is a tree nymph that is a female spirit of a tree, in Greek mythology. In Greek 'drys' signifies "oak". Thus dryads are specifically the nymphs of oak trees, though the term has come to be used for all tree nymphs in general.*

Pixie Day is an old tradition which takes place annually in the East Devon town of Ottery St. Mary in June. The day commemorates a legend of pixies being banished from the town to local caves known as the 'Pixie's Parlour'

POLAROID

7870/118522

A somewhat,
albeit not impossible,
difficult spell to perform: however it
is easiest to perform in Autumn/Fall. In order
to evoke the power of this spell you must catch
a falling leaf before it touches the ground. The leaf
has spent its existence upon the branch, which is in turn
part of the tree whose roots entwine with Mother Earth
and by catching it the leaf has not completed the great
circle and therefore has power. When you catch it, hold
the leaf between flattened palms and say the following.

Keep those that I love and those that love me
Safe as we travel between wherever it may be,

I feel your power surge between my hands
And now return you freely to these woodlands.

Now place the leaf upon the ground. Feel the power of
nature as you complete this final journey of this trees
offspring, from its lifelong perch to its return to the soil
from whence its essence came. This is the force that
will protect you and your loved ones on the
journeys you will make. Do this
annually as a mark of respect for
the power of nature.

The season's
palette makes aglow
Through the wonder and
splendour of every tree
Both root and twig in
opposition grow,
Does the Green Man's
spirit reside
in thee?

# STRENGTH AND PROTECTION

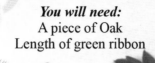

***You will need:***
A piece of Oak
Length of green ribbon

Green Man carving at
Cathédrale Saint-Pierre de Poitiers

The Green-Man
is also a
popular name
for English
public houses

The Green Man ~ Usually referred to in works
on architecture as foliate heads or foliate masks,
carvings of the Green Man may take many forms,
naturalistic or decorative. The simplest depict a
man's face peering out of dense foliage. Some may
have leaves for hair, perhaps with a leafy beard.

Take a piece of oak;
this can be a twig, a leaf or even an acorn.
All are the embodiment of the oak and contain
the spirit and strength of this mighty tree. Bind the
green ribbon around the piece of oak whilst reciting
the following; this will evoke the spirit of
the oak king.

The seed that grows

The tree that follows

The branches that spread

And the leaves that fall,

Mighty Oak king we do beseech

In our hearts let your strength reach.

Afterwards, unbind your amulet and bury it in the soil,
this will ground the spell. If you used an acorn then you
might be lucky enough to start the growth of a new oak
tree, thereby ensuring that the cycle of life begins anew.

Alternatively, you can plait your ribbon and
keep it as a reminder of the spell and
of the strength obtained
from the oak.

On

the opiate nights

betwixt crescent and full

Stand alone atop the

knoll of knights interred,

With ceremonial athame

and gifts in hand

Make your offerings to

the winged guardian

on high.

# TO EMPOWER A TALISMAN

***You will need:***
A pendant or similar

In Greek mythology, the sun god was originally Helios and the moon goddess Selene, but over time, this changed. Artemis came to be associated with Selene, just like Apollo with Helios. Apollo became a sun god and Artemis became the goddess of the moon.

A dragon is a mythological representation of a reptile. In ancient times, dragons were mostly envisaged as serpents, but since the Middle Ages, it became common to depict them with legs, resembling a lizard. Today we see Dragons depicted mostly as a huge lizard, or a snake with two pairs of lizard~type legs, and able to emit fire from their mouths. The European dragon has bat~like wings growing from its back.

A talisman worn
around the neck can serve
both as a protection from evil
as well as channelling positive energy
to the wearer. First, you need to take an item
or symbol that means something special to you.
This can be a bought pendant or something that
you may have made yourself, a homemade charm
for instance. The moon's gravity has a powerful
effect on our earth; it makes its orbit stable and
controls the flow of the tides. Power of moon-
light can be utilized to enhance protection.
Take your talisman out on a moonlit night and
holding aloft say the following:

Moon that shines down this night
Bless this offering with your light,

May your power enter and stay
And keep all that is evil far away,

Calling across the night I ask this of you
And give thanks for the wonders you do

Blessed be.

Envisage the power of the moon flowing
into your talisman and sealing
the protection.

With

my eye to the

bright heavens

My thoughts drift through

the voids of space,

And in my mind race

a thousand questions

For answers waiting

shall I stay in

this place.

# FINDING THE
# ANSWER WITHIN

***You will need:***
Amethyst crystal
Incense (Lotus)

Most ancient civilizations saw pictures in the stars of the night sky. The earliest known efforts to catalogue the stars date to Cuneiform (*It is one of the earliest known forms of written expression*) texts and artefacts dating back roughly 6000 years. These remnants, found in the valley of the Euphrates River, suggest that the ancients observing the heavens saw the lion, the bull and the scorpion in the stars.

✳ In ancient Rome wine was served in amethyst goblets; the purple stone enhanced the colour of the wine making it possible for servants to water it down.

✳ Knights on the crusade loved amethyst and attached it their rosaries as magical protection

Only too often
do others look to us for answers,
whether as confidante, to settle an argument
etc. Yet the most important questions we save for
ourselves and sometimes they're bigger than us,
as it were, and so this spell will help you find the
answer within yourself. It can be formed either
outside or indoors *(depending on the weather)*.

Light incense to create the mood. On a clear
night look up at the stars and pick a particular
star or constellation. Hold the crystal aloft in
both hands as you are gazing up and
repeat the following three times:

Bright star I call upon you now

Your essence in this stone reside,

Grant me power to know how

And in this matter be my guide.

By the power of three so mote it be!

In your current state of serenity hold the charged
crystal to your heart. Feel the solution to your
question become clear. The crystal will not hold
the energy for extended periods so you
must perform this from time to
time to keep it
energised.

Many thought
themselves the bravest
of the brave
They dared to enter
unbidden to my lair,
Remorseless I sent each
to their grave
So heed my warning
and around me take
your care.

# ATTRACTING WEALTH

***You will need:***
Three golden coins.
An item of clothing with
pockets.

In the age of men
and dragons, peace between
the two was made with
offerings of gold and not
as fairy tales would
have us believe virginal
sacrifices. Dragons were
the imparters of wisdom
and guidance as well as protecting the virtues of
young maidens entrusted to them, requesting gold
as payment in all transactions.

For they alone knew the true mystical value of
the Earth Goddesses most beautiful mineral. It
wasn't in its rarity but the power it instilled in the
owner, hence why they relished in guarding their
horde voraciously.

This spell
can be used at any time
to attract success; however, its power
can be increased if performed in the light of a
full moon. Take three golden coins and turn them in
your pocket while looking up into the night sky and
chanting the spell three times. The coins will receive the
attracting power of the moon and stars to
increase your wealth.

Three golden coins spin riches bright
A web of wealth on this dark night

From night skies ancient mystery
Comes money and prosperity

Venus, Jupiter, Moon and Mars
Abundance shines from countless stars

I chant this spell three times three
Great wealth be mine so mote it be!

Keep the three golden coins in a safe place until
you become wealthy. Then throw them into
the night, to give thanks for the help of
the moon and stars.

Behold this moment
daughter of mine
These grains count the
span of man,
Duty is given through
our bloodline
One that precedes when
time began.

# STITCH IN TIME

***You will need:***
Sand timer
Needle & sewing thread.

DEATH | XIII | DER TOD

LA MORT | LA MUERTE

Unlike most other methods of measuring time the hourglass concretely represents the present as being between the past and the future, and this has made it an enduring symbol of time itself

In Tarot, death does not necessarily indicate physical death. This card simply denotes transformation and change. It is a time of deep transformation and is likely to be both inner and outwardly in your life. Situations, things and people that you have counted on or become used to, may no longer be available to you in quite the same way as they once were.

This spell utilizes the power of time, to be more accurate, empowering oneself from a moment in our past in which we were able to deal with a particular situation. It's an ideal spell for job interviews or similar.

Recall a special moment in your life, either one with joy unequalled or one in which you had control of a bad situation. Now, relate a colour with that experience; it's surprising how easy it is to do when we try. For colour, like the sense of smell is a great medium for recollection. The colour could be of something we were wearing (*particularly strong*), someone else wore or just the colour of the sky on that occasion. For whatever reason this is the colour needed for this spell, so now choose similar cotton thread. Turn over the sand timer and begin to sew a small dot of thread somewhere inconspicuous (*lapel, sleeve cuff etc.*) whilst saying the following three times:

From across the ages I call to thee
And weave thy power unto me,
Strengthen my will that I may see
My confidence this day as it should be,
So mote it be!

From now on whenever you rub this sewn token you will be empowered with strength and confidence from a time that you thought long gone.

Be

careful just what

you wish for

The power is mine to

make it real,

Make me an offer that

I cannot ignore

All I ask is that

you remain forever

loyal.

# BINDING SPELL

***You will need:***
Cord, ribbon
or natural fibre

It is believed that numbers contain magical powers that can be invoked by using certain sacred ratios and shapes. Each number has a particular significance that must be fully understood when casting spells. This spell uses the number 3.

## 3 THE TRINITY AND THE SACRED TRIANGLE; FERTILITY, CREATION AND BALANCE

The tying and untying of knots is used to bind, enforce and release energy in many spells. In ancient Egypt it was believed that a magic knot was the points at which the forces converge that unite the divine and the human world. Therefore a knot tied on earth was also tied in heaven.

*This spell is to
guard against harassment or ill intent
from another person and should be only
performed with care and understanding of the
warning at the beginning of
this book.*

Take your chosen piece of cord and prepare to make
three knots into it; say the following as you do so:

## First knot binds purpose,
## Second knot binds the ill-wish,
## Third knot seals the spell,
## Until all the knots are undone.

As you say the verse, tie the corresponding knot and think
about what you are binding into it. This will stop whatever
it is from doing harm. Once complete, place the knotted
item somewhere safe that you will remember where
you placed it. For once the threat has passed it
is very important to untie all the knots
before discarding.

To seek her
be there at dawn's
first light
With gown of chastity and
beating pure heart,
In the midst of the cedar trees
and apples so ripe
Behold the most wondrous
and magical of
sights.

# DISPEL BAD DREAMS

***You will need:***
A Dream Catcher
Wine glass
Incense (*lavender*)

**SELENE** *was the Titan goddess of the moon. She was depicted as a woman either riding side saddle on a horse or in a chariot drawn by a pair of winged steeds. Her lunar sphere or crescent was represented as either a crown set upon her head or as the fold of a raised, shining cloak..*

If you are troubled with bad dreams or nightmares then this spell will help to keep your dreams good and the nightmares away. To aid you into a relaxed state light the incense and draw a star in the air over the dream catcher with the smoke and say:

# Fair beings of light,
# So good and so bright
# Guide only blessed dreams tonight

Secondly, draw a circle around the star, again with the incense, and say:

# Visions in the night,
# Be playful and fun
# Keep the bad dreams on the run.

Place the incense down safely, now hold your hands over the dream catcher, and imagine only good feelings flowing out of your hands and into the dream catcher. When relaxed and you feel the moment is right, be ready to tap the glass gently with a pen or similar and say the following:

# Goddess of the moon hear my plea
# With one single clear note I send to thee,
*(tap the glass)*
# With a second that it may guide you to me,
*(tap the glass)*
# A third that only good dreams shall I see,

Tap glass and let the incense burn out. Now you can hang the dream catcher at the head of your bed and dream only pleasant dreams knowing that any other kind are caught within it.

I humbly
kneel and do beseech
Empower this instrument
with your might,
That my arm may
extend its reach
To smite thy foes and
bring them to
the light.

# EMPOWER THYSELF

***You will need:***
Candle
Bowl of water
Salt
Incense (*sandalwood*).

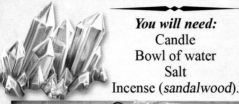

The Greek classical elements also included a '*fifth*' element, Aether, meaning pure, fresh air or clear sky, imagined in Greek mythology to be the pure essence where the gods lived and which they breathed, different to the air breathed by mortals.

The twelve signs of the zodiac are divided into the four elements:

Air signs are Gemini, Libra and Aquarius
Fire signs are Aries, Leo and Sagittarius
Water signs are Cancer, Scorpio, and Pisces
Earth signs are Taurus, Virgo and Capricorn

To understand the elements
and their place in the cycle of life is to
understand the balance between them, which
empowers and brings greater spiritual channelling.
Here you call upon the elements saying:

Air: The air we breathe, the wind, new beginnings,
Fire: The Sun, the warmth of heat, loving passion,
Water: The Rivers and oceans, the tide, emotions,
Earth: The rocks, ground we walk on, our support,

Use the candle flame to light the incense and thereby
your passion to start a new beginning. Sprinkle the salt
onto the water in the bowl and stir in until dissolved,
saying the following as you do so:

Allow these crystals to start anew
Power combined will now accrue,
Allow me to face my flaws clearly,
By the power of the elements –
so mote it be!

All the elements have been combined and thanks
given, you have given your psyche the
support to deal with any emotional
weaknesses.

# INDEX OF PAINTINGS

For more information about these paintings and to see more of Anne's art visit www.annestokes.com

# INDEX OF SPELLS

# NOTES

You have the lock,
You are the key,
Release the power,
So mote it be.